ROBOT AND DRONE TECHNOLOGY

BY AMY C. REA

childsworld.com

ABOUT THE AUTHOR
Amy C. Rea is the author of several children's books. She also writes about travel and food. She lives in St. Anthony, Minnesota, with her husband and silly dog.

Published by The Child's World®
800-599-READ • www.childsworld.com

Copyright © 2024 by The Child's World®
All rights reserved. No part of this book may be reproduced or utilized in any form or by any means without written permission from the publisher.

Photography Credits
Photographs ©: Josh Reynolds/AP Images, cover, 1; iStockphoto, 5, 22; Agence Meurisse/National Library of France/Gallica, 6; Magic Orb Studio/Shutterstock Images, 9; US Air Force/National Museum of the US Air Force, 10, 12; Mass Communication Specialist 2nd Class Stuart Phillips/Defense Imagery Management Operations Center/US Navy/DVIDS, 13; John Pratt/Keystone Features/Hulton Archive/Getty Images, 14; Shutterstock Images, 17, 21; Aleksandra Suzi/Shutterstock Images, 18; Red Line Editorial, 25; Mike Dotta/Shutterstock Images, 26; Senior Airman John Ennis/48th Fighter Wing Public Affairs/US Air Force/DVIDS, 28

ISBN Information
9781503869851 (Reinforced Library Binding)
9781503881327 (Portable Document Format)
9781503882638 (Online Multi-user eBook)
9781503883949 (Electronic Publication)

LCCN 2022951244

Printed in the United States of America

CONTENTS

FAST FACTS 4

CHAPTER ONE
TAKING FLIGHT 7

CHAPTER TWO
PILOTLESS AIRCRAFT 10

CHAPTER THREE
ROBOTS THAT MOVE ON THEIR OWN 15

CHAPTER FOUR
PICK-AND-PLACE ROBOTS 19

CHAPTER FIVE
EVERYDAY DRONES 22

CHAPTER SIX
SPOT, THE ROBOT DOG 27

Think About It 29
Glossary 30
Selected Bibliography 31
Find Out More 31
Index 32

FAST FACTS

- In 1907, two brothers in France invented a quadcopter, a flying machine with four **rotors**. Similar technology would later be used in **drones**.
- In 1917, Archibald Low built the first pilotless aircraft for use in World War I (1914–1918). It did not work very well, but other **engineers** used his work to develop drones that did work.
- In 1949, William Grey Walter created the first robot that could move by itself and find its way around obstacles. Walter's technology is still used in modern robots.
- In 1978, Hiroshi Makino developed a pick-and-place robot that could be used in factories. Pick-and-place robots began working in the early 1980s.
- In 2010, researchers used tiny electronics and sensors to develop drones that were inexpensive. These drones became popular for both business and entertainment.
- In 2015, Boston Dynamics invented a robot dog named Spot. It was the most advanced robot of its time.

Today, everyday people can use robots and drones. People may even build their own.

CHAPTER ONE

TAKING FLIGHT

It was 1907 in France, and a group of men stood in an empty field. Two brothers, Jacques and Louis Breguet, had created a new flying machine. Some of the other men were there to help test it. Some were there to watch. The flying machine had a center area where a pilot sat. There were four arms going out from the pilot's seat. Every arm had a rotor. The rotors each had a set of blades that looked like a plus sign. The men held their breath, hoping the machine would lift off the ground.

The pilot was in place. He started the motors. The rotors started spinning. The machine slowly lifted into the air, just as the brothers hoped it would. But the machine began wobbling after lifting only 2 feet (.6 m) off the ground. The brothers and two assistants rushed forward to hold it steady.

◀ **Louis Breguet invented many kinds of aircraft, including planes and helicopters.**

Their machine did not go far. But it was the first to use technology that would later be used to build drones and helicopters.

The flying machine they built was called the Gyroplane. It was powered by motors. The rotor on each of its four arms had blades like a fan's. Two of the rotors turned in one direction. The other two turned in the opposite direction. When they spun, the rotors lifted the machine off the ground. This was different from airplanes, which had to drive down a runway to gain speed before taking off.

The Gyroplane also needed a pilot. But even before its invention, people had shown interest in creating a machine that could fly without one. There was military interest in using pilotless aircraft as weapons. The Gyroplane would never be developed into a pilotless aircraft. But it would inspire future flying machines that didn't need pilots.

The design of the Gyroplane is also called a quadcopter because the flying machine had four rotors. Other early helicopters used this design, too. Eventually, helicopters would be created that only needed one or two rotors. The quadcopter design would still prove useful, though. It was simple and kept aircraft stable. Modern small drones are often quadcopters.

▲ **Many modern drones use a quadcopter design.**

But inventors had to make many other advances in technology before these aircraft became widely available.

CHAPTER TWO

PILOTLESS AIRCRAFT

It was 1917, and an engineer named Archibald Low was working on a military base in England. The United Kingdom was in the middle of World War I. Military pilots were leading bombing raids across Germany. These bombing flights were dangerous. A pilot could be shot down by an enemy in the air.

◀ **The Kettering Bug was successfully flown in 1918, just over one year after Archibald Low tested his drone.**

Low designed something he hoped would help his country. He came up with a way for planes to fly without pilots. The plane would be controlled by a radio **guidance** system he built.

Once Low built the pilotless plane, he and his team took it to a military base. Low handed the controls to a fighter pilot named Henry Segrave. They launched the plane. Low's radio guidance system worked. Segrave was able to control the plane for a short time. The plane did a loop, and Segrave cheered. Then it crashed. However, it flew long enough to show that Low's idea worked.

That same year, US Army engineers started working on a similar remote-controlled plane. They called their version the Kettering Bug. It was smaller than other airplanes. The Army launched the plane from a cart that ran down a track. The Bug could reach speeds up to 120 miles per hour (190 kmh). It could fly 75 miles (120 km). When it came close to the target, the engine would shut off. The Bug then dropped to the ground and exploded with 180 pounds (82 kg) of bombs. However, the Bug was never used in battle. World War I ended before any pilotless plane was reliable enough to be used in combat.

▲ A Radioplane OQ-2A is displayed in the National Museum of the US Air Force in Greene County, Ohio.

The British invented a machine in 1935 called a target drone. This was the first time a pilotless aircraft was called a drone. The word *drone* described the noise the machines made. They sounded like a swarm of bees.

During World War II (1939–1945), the Germans created a drone called the V-1 flying bomb. It exploded when it reached a target. The US military built its own drone called the Radioplane OQ-2. Unlike the V-1, it was not a weapon. It was a target drone.

▲ The US military still uses target drones today. The BQM-74E is one modern target drone.

Troops practiced shooting weapons by aiming at the drone. During World War II, the United States made almost 1,000 drones for military use.

More technological advances would be needed before drones would be cheap and useful enough for businesses and everyday people. For many decades, drones were mostly used by the military. Today, the US military continues to use many kinds of drones. Some gather information about enemies and others are used for combat.

CHAPTER THREE

ROBOTS THAT MOVE ON THEIR OWN

In 1949, inventor William Grey Walter kneeled in his laboratory. He pointed a remote control at his latest invention. It was a robot that could move freely around the lab without running into things. It could **navigate** its way back to its charging station without help, too. No one had successfully built a robot like this before. His robot looked like a construction worker's hard hat. A little tube coming out of the top looked from side to side. This sensor helped the robot know where to move. The robot was not fast, but it could move on its own.

Walter's little robot blob seems very old-fashioned today. But the technology he used to help it move and sense its surroundings set the stage for modern-day robots. Many modern robots use newer forms of the same technology.

◄ **William Grey Walter's robots were sometimes called tortoises because of their shape.**

The sensor developed for Walter's invention is still in use. A sensor is a device that can recognize light, sound, and other things in its environment. A **processor** uses that information to control the robot's movements. This is similar to how humans use senses, such as sight and touch, to provide information to the brain. The brain then decides how to respond.

Communication between sensors and processors is called a **feedback loop**. As the robot moves, its sensors continue to detect information. The processor continues to tell the robot what to do. For example, if something is in the robot's path, it recognizes the object. It processes that information and changes its route. Once the robot moves in a new direction, its sensors continue to look out for objects. If they sense another obstacle, the processor will tell the robot to change its route again. This process repeats while the robot is running.

Modern robots look much different than Walter's did. They have advanced technology that allows them to complete much more complicated tasks. But the basic technology from Walter's robot is still used in robots today.

Vacuuming robots, such as the iRobot and Roomba, use feedback loops. This helps the robots avoid obstacles. ▶

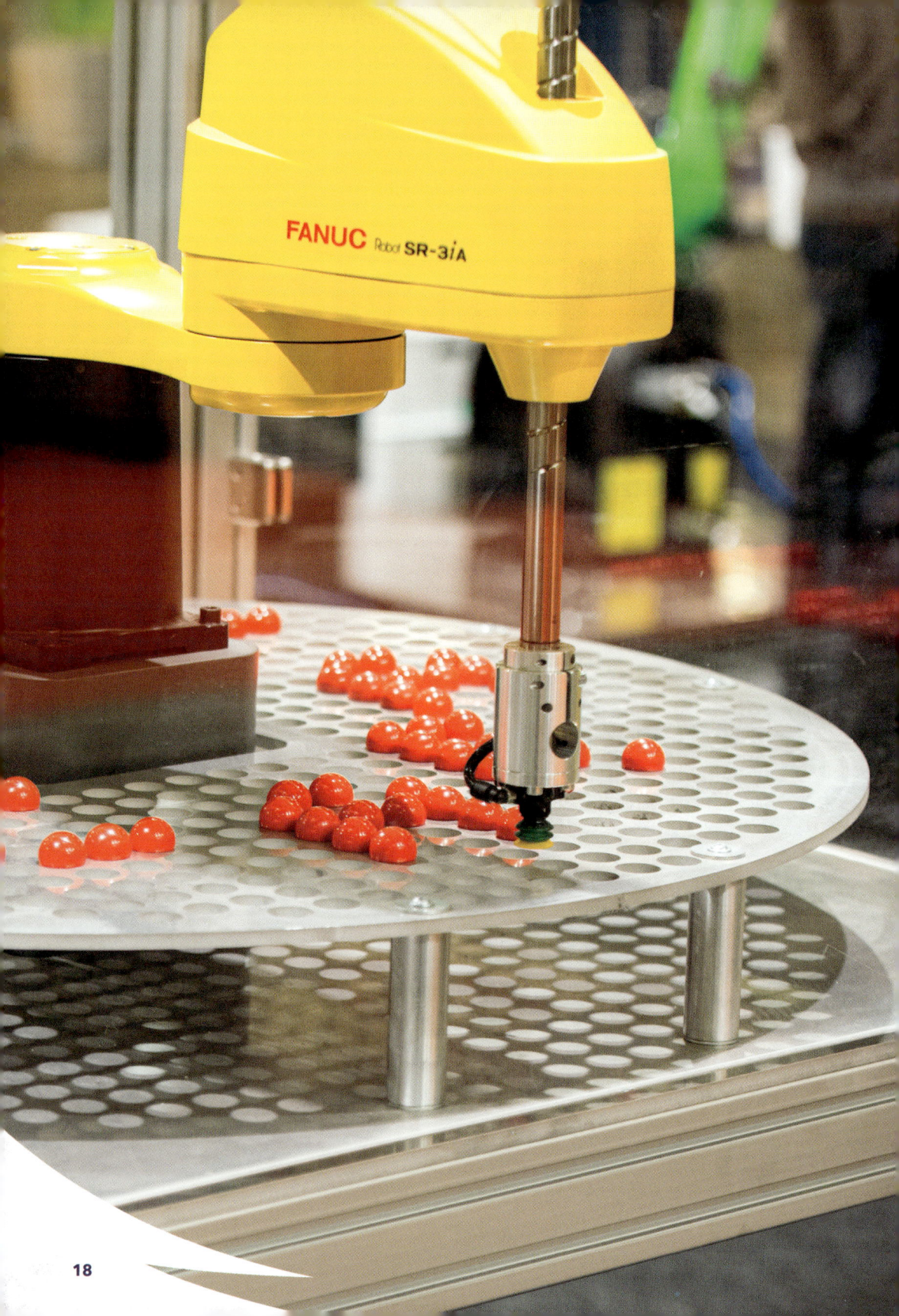

CHAPTER FOUR

PICK-AND-PLACE ROBOTS

In 1978, Hiroshi Makino was working in his lab in Japan. He had an idea. Robots had come a long way from little boxes that could move around on the floor. Engineers had created robotic arms that could lift and stack things at factories. They were very popular at car **manufacturers**.

Makino thought robots could do more. He had recently attended a meeting where people from all over the world showed new developments in robot technology. The robots he saw were strong, but they were not very fast or efficient. Inspired by their designs, he thought he could design a robot that could move much more quickly and with greater accuracy. Makino wanted to design a robot that could quickly pick up small pieces and put them where they needed to be. This robot would change manufacturing.

◀ Robotic arms inspired by Hiroshi Makino's invention became more efficient and accurate as technology advanced.

His invention was called the Selective Compliance Assembly Robot Arm (SCARA). In the 1980s, many manufacturers began using SCARA robots. The robots were very precise. They did not move around the factory floor. Instead, they were set in place. They could turn from side to side. They could pick up small parts and put them in exactly the right place. SCARA robots quickly became known as "pick-and-place" robots. They were helpful for companies using small electronic pieces. Things like computer chips and watches could be made much more quickly because of this technology.

This invention is still used today. The robots have sped up manufacturing processes and reduced costs for the manufacturers. SCARA robots are used mostly by factories that make cars, electronics, medicines, and cosmetics. They are also used in medical manufacturing for things such as hearing aids.

Other researchers used the pick-and-place technology to develop robots that are used in surgery. These types of robots can help doctors perform difficult operations. Many surgical robots have one arm with a camera. These cameras provide a clearer and more detailed view than the surgeon's eyes alone. The other arm holds surgical instruments. The surgeon controls this arm. Using a robot helps the surgeon be more precise and controlled.

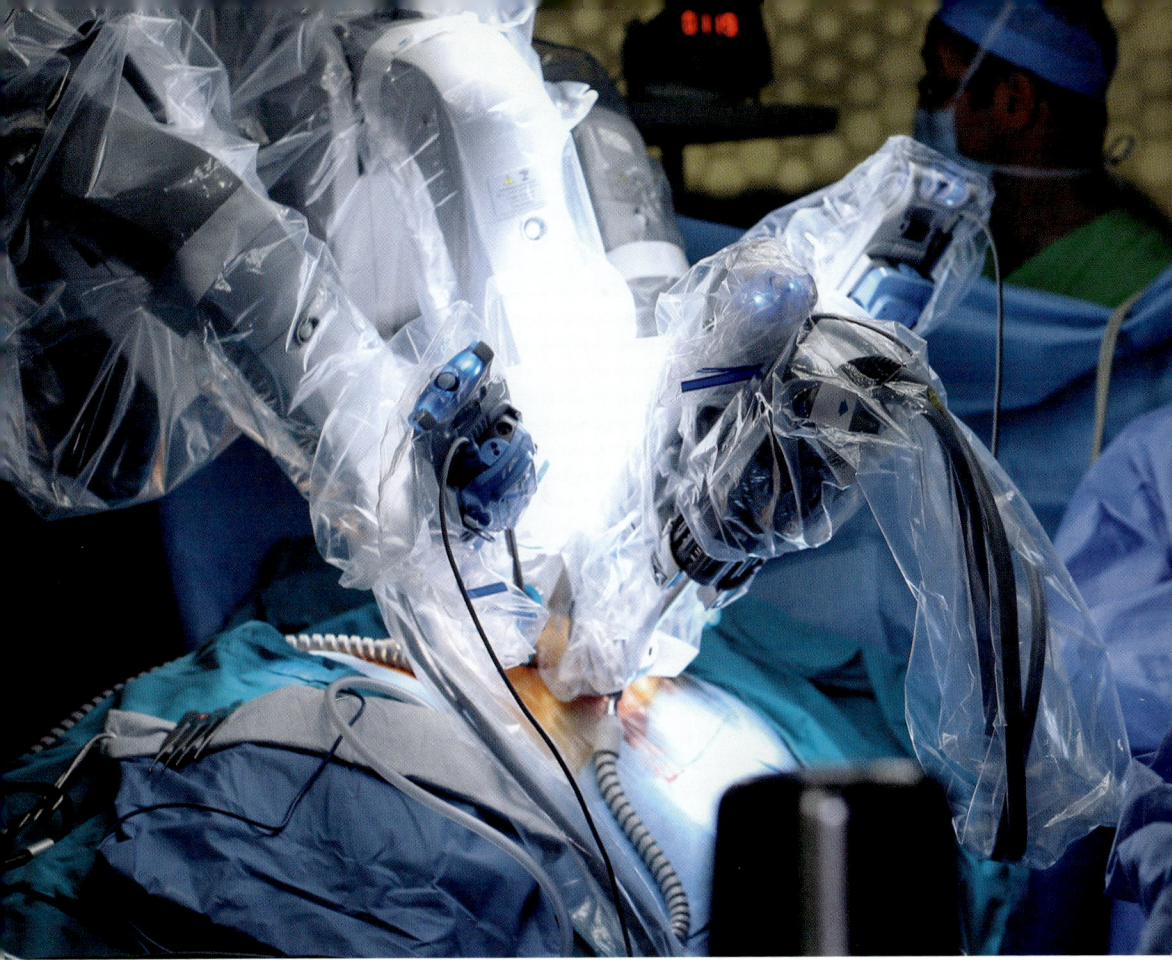

▲ **Da Vinci Surgical Systems are one kind of medical robot. Like SCARA robots, they use robotic arms to assist doctors.**

SCARA robots are quick, precise, and consistent. This makes them helpful for lots of different tasks. Engineers are always developing new robots and finding new, creative uses for SCARA technology.

CHAPTER FIVE

EVERYDAY DRONES

A team of researchers in France checked the Wi-Fi on their smartphones. They were about to test a new drone. It was 2010, and this was one of the smallest drones ever made. The drone was a small quadcopter. The drone's body was long and slim. Four rotors extended from its sides.

◀ **The Parrot AR.Drone could be controlled from up to 164 feet (50 m) away.**

A piece could be added that went around all four rotors. If the drone ran into something, it would bounce off. The rotors would not be damaged. With this piece, the drone was 28 inches (71 cm) long and wide. It weighed less than 1 pound (.45 kg). The drone could be easily controlled using a smartphone. One of the researchers used his phone to start the drone. It took off and flew away.

The French company was called Parrot. They named this new drone the Parrot AR.Drone. It was a huge success. Parrot won awards and sold more than 120,000 drones in under a year. The AR.Drone was easy to use and available to regular people, not just the military. When it was first released, each AR.Drone cost about $300.

A big reason for its popularity was its size. It was smaller than previous drones. Parrot used electronics that were much smaller than previous versions. That meant Parrot's drones were less expensive to manufacture and less expensive for the public to buy.

The shrinking of the drone's pieces happened partly because smartphones increased in popularity. Drones use some of the same parts as smartphones, such as sensors and batteries.

These parts continued to get smaller, better, and cheaper during the early 2010s. Drones became easier to manage and more reliable.

By that time, drone technology had already come a long way since Archibald Low's first remote-piloted aircraft. The Kettering Bug and the V-1 were important first steps in military drone technology. Military drones had become powerful tools for combat and gathering information about enemies.

But Parrot helped show that drones did not need to be confined to military use. As a result of advancements in drones made for everyday people, modern drones are used for many different things. Scientists use them for research. Drones can track and identify different animals and plants. They can track storms and monitor rivers to predict flooding. Drones also help speed up disaster recovery efforts by providing quick views of disaster areas and delivering necessary supplies.

Workers in the energy industry use drones to check on gas and oil pipelines as well as wind and solar farms. Farmers use drones to monitor their crops. Law enforcement uses them for safety at large public gatherings. People use them for photography and other outdoor entertainment, too.

In the future, more businesses may use drones to deliver packages. Drones are being engineered to carry more weight.

This will make it easier for companies to use them for deliveries. New drones are being manufactured regularly. In the years to come, there will likely be many changes in the world of drones.

STEERING A QUADCOPTER

Two rotors on a quadcopter drone turn one way. The other two rotors turn the opposite way. A pilot can change the speed of each rotor to steer the drone.

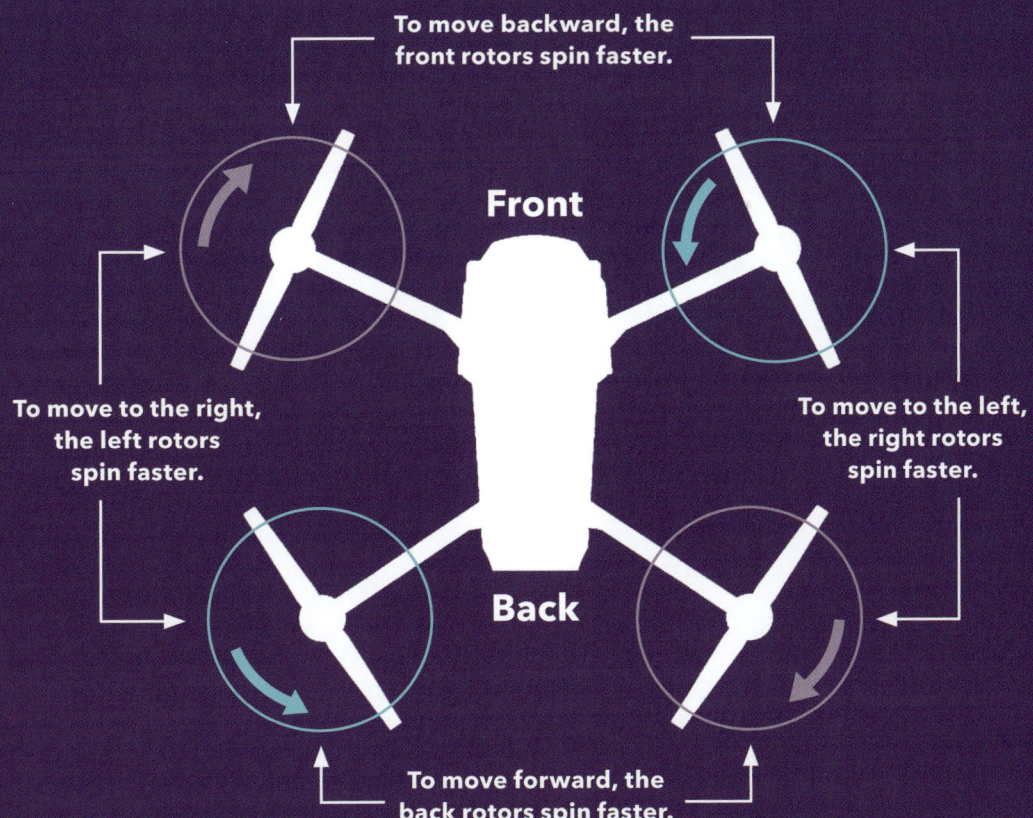

CHAPTER SIX

SPOT, THE ROBOT DOG

A team of researchers in Massachusetts was ready to test its latest development: a robot dog named Spot. They worked at Boston Dynamics, which had built other robot dogs before. But this new model was designed to move around more freely than the earlier versions. It was also much smaller and lighter than the first robot dogs. That meant it would be easier to transport and handle.

In 2015, an engineer turned Spot on. The robot dog began to move on its four legs, just like a real dog. The researchers watched as Spot walked through their office, navigating obstacles. A researcher pushed Spot, but it didn't fall over. It quickly readjusted and kept walking. They watched Spot easily climb a staircase. Then it walked up a hill, racing an older robot.

◀ Scientists can attach cameras, microphones, sensors, and other types of equipment to Spot.

▲ **Spot has been tested during military training missions. It can help soldiers stay safe by giving them more information about their surroundings.**

Spot clearly won. Spot was everything the researchers had hoped for.

Boston Dynamics continued to develop new versions of Spot. As its technology advanced, Spot learned to do many things. It could open doors and bring a drink to a human, like a real dog could fetch a ball and bring it back. Spot could even dance. It had an advanced navigation system, too.

Since then, Spot has proven to be much more than a really cool pet. Spot can make workplaces safer by doing specific tasks that might put humans at risk. The robot can inspect places that are dangerous or difficult for humans to access.

It can gather important data. NASA worked with partners to develop a version of Spot. Eventually, it might be used to explore caves on other planets.

The ability to move easily is not Spot's only benefit. New versions of Spot can carry up to 30 pounds (14 kg) of equipment. The robot is used for warehouse work, moving items around to help packers. In the early 2020s, the French military tested Spot for use in combat. The military may use Spot to check out bombs or bring soldiers the supplies they need.

Some people think Spot is a glimpse into the future. Its technology is much more advanced than William Grey Walter's 1949 robots or Hiroshi Makino's pick-and-place arms. With advances in technology, robots will continue to be stronger, more efficient, and able to do more complex tasks.

THINK ABOUT IT

▶ What do you think are the most important uses for drones and robots today?
▶ Have robots or drones impacted your life? If so, explain how.
▶ What would you like drones and robots to be able to do in the future? Explain how that would benefit people.

GLOSSARY

drones (DROHNZ): Drones are aircraft that are controlled with a remote and have no people on board. The military uses many kinds of drones.

engineers (en-juh-NEERZ): Engineers are people who design and build things such as machines. Archibald Low and other engineers made some of the first military drones.

feedback loop (FEED-bak LOOP): A feedback loop is a repeated process where information is gathered and then used to make a decision. The robot used a feedback loop to sense obstacles and move around them.

guidance (GUY-dunss): Guidance means to direct someone or something in a specific direction. Archibald Low invented the first drone with a radio guidance system.

manufacturers (man-yoo-FAK-chur-urz): Manufacturers build things using machinery. Manufacturers use robots to build things more efficiently.

navigate (NA-vuh-gayt): To navigate is to follow a specific route to get from one location to another. The robot dog Spot can navigate around obstacles.

processor (PRAH-ses-ur): A processor is the central part of a computer that takes actions to achieve a specific outcome. A drone uses a processor like the kind used in a smartphone.

rotors (ROH-turs): Rotors are mechanical parts that spin. Rotors with blades attached allow quadcopters to fly.

SELECTED BIBLIOGRAPHY

Ghaffarzadeh, Khasha. "New Robotics and Drones 2018–2038." *IDTechEx*, idtechex.com, n.d. Accessed 17 Nov. 2022.

"Spot." *Boston Dynamics*. bostondynamics.com, n.d. Accessed 17 Nov. 2022.

Vyas, Kashyap. "A Brief History of Drones." *Interesting Engineering*, 29 June 2020, interestingengineering.com. Accessed 28 Nov. 2022.

FIND OUT MORE

BOOKS

Buller, Laura, et al. *Robot.* New York, NY: DK Publishing, 2018.

Drimmer, Stephanie Warren. *Ultimate Book of the Future.* Washington, DC: National Geographic Kids, 2022.

Henzel, Cynthia Kennedy. *Powerful Military Drones.* Parker, CO: The Child's World, 2024.

WEBSITES

Visit our website for links about robots and drones: **childsworld.com/links**

Note to Parents, Caregivers, Teachers, and Librarians: We routinely verify our Web links to make sure they are safe and active sites. So encourage your readers to check them out!

INDEX

AR.Drone, 22–23

Boston Dynamics, 27–28
Breguet, Jacques, 7
Breguet, Louis, 7

delivery drones, 24–25

engineers, 10, 11, 19, 21, 27

feedback loop, 16

Germany, 10
Gyroplane, 7–8

helicopters, 8

Kettering Bug, 11, 24

Low, Archibald, 10–11, 24

Makino, Hiroshi, 19, 29
manufacturing, 19–20
military drones, 8, 11–13, 24

NASA, 29

Parrot, 22–24
pick-and-place robots, 19–21, 29
pilot, 7–8, 10–11, 25
processor, 16

quadcopter, 8, 22, 25

radio guidance system, 11
Radioplane OQ-2, 12–13
remote control, 11, 15, 24
rotors, 7–8, 22–23, 25

Segrave, Henry, 11
Selective Compliance Assembly Robot Arm (SCARA), 20–21
sensors, 15–16, 23
smartphones, 22–23
Spot, 27–29
steering, 25
surgical robots, 20

target drone, 12–13

United Kingdom, 10
US military, 11, 13

V-1 flying bomb, 12, 24

Walter, William Grey, 15–16, 29
World War I, 10–11
World War II, 12–13